Mathematical Challenges for a KS2 classroom

Mike Ollerton

Pick and Mix
Mathematical Challenges for a KS2 classroom

This book is a collection of tasks I have assembled for learners in KS2.

I was prompted to do this by some voluntary mathematics teaching I have been doing at a local primary school, Grayrigg in South Cumbria.

The children I work with are in a mixed Y3 to Y6 class so the issue of differentiated learning is ever present; though it is not merely age related as the mathematics some younger children engage with is at a higher level of cognition than some of the older children.

As we know, teaching and learning are highly complex activities and there are no easy solutions or ways of teaching that are guaranteed to motivate or enable success, for all of the children, all of the time. Knowing this, however, does not stop us from trying. *Hope springs eternal!*

Pedagogically, the ideas arise from creating three week units of work all of which begin with common starting-off lessons. Apart from the Geometry unit, which requires special equipment (9-pin geoboards) I have not suggested what these starting-off lessons might look like; I would not wish to suggest I could. What I offer are sequences of problem-based challenges to follow them that children can work with and develop as far as they are able.

I make no suggestion whether these are individual or collaborative tasks.

The challenges are organised under the following headings:

- Addition and differencing
- Number and Place Value
- Mainly Multiplication
- Number chains
- Calculations using +, −, ×, ÷ and brackets
- Measures
- Geometry
- Algebra
- Miscellany

Some of the ideas I have taken from the ATM publication "Eight days a week". Others are of my own invention and other are from who knows where – mists of time and all that.

I offer around 100 challenges across the nine areas listed above. They are inevitably just a starting point as new ideas surface and become favourites, as these have done.

A set of slides is available to purchase separately for presenting the challenges in the classroom.

Mike

Contents

Pick and Mix – Mathematical Challenges for a KS2 classroom

1 – Addition and differencing

A Cuisenaire problem	4
Making 10	4
Coins	4
Common triangle totals 1	4
Common triangle totals 2	5
Dartboard totals	5
Domino challenge 1 i), ii)	5
Domino challenge 2 i), ii), iii)	5
Domino challenge 3 i), ii)	6
Domino challenge 4 i), ii), iii)	6
Dominoes and differencing 1	6
Dominoes and differencing 2	7
Dominoes and differencing 3	7
Maximum difference game	7
Pairing and squaring	7
Making amounts of money	8
Number grid problem	8

2 – Number and Place Value

Number cards 1	9
Number cards 2	9
Reading numbers	9
Number of 1s	9
Number cards 3	10
Number of millimetres	10
Strange but is it true?	10
Exponential growth	10
Working with decimals 1	11
Working with decimals 2	11
Working with decimals 3	11

3 – Mainly multiplication

A two dice problem	12
Listing factors	12
Max factor	12
Factor chains	12
The highest LCM problem	13
Factors and consecutive sums	13
Partitioning and multiplying	13
Multiplication facts	14
Multiplying consecutive numbers	14
More multiplying consecutive numbers	14
Another multiplication marvel	14
Largest product	15
Addition and multiplication	15
Number of words in your story book	15
Birth date values	15

4 – Number chains

Number chain 1	16
Number chain 2	16
Number chain 3	16
Number chain 4	17

5 – Calculations using +, –, ×, ÷ and brackets

Making up calculations 1	17
Making up calculations 2	17
Making up calculations 3	18
Making up calculations 4	18
Six 6s	18
Seven 7s	18
The four dice challenge	19

6 – Measures

Digital clocks	20
One handed clocks	20
Times before noon	21
Distance around your head	21
Height and arm span	21
Middle of a year	21
I have a good friend who lives in Falmouth	21
Scale drawing	21
Time	21
Date and time	22
Weighing things up	22
How much is your name worth	22
Weight of water	22
One million minutes	22
A hearty question	22
Hour and minute hands	22

7 – Algebra

Think of a number	23
Algebra and addition 1	23
Algebra and addition 2	23
Algebra and fractions	24

8 – Miscellany

Making 5 with Cuisenaire	25
Making 15	25
Cuisenaire and area	25
Dominoes and the game of 3s and 2s	26
Dominoes and the game of 5s and 3s	26
Guzintas	27
Summing consecutive numbers	27
Calculator challenge 1	27
Calculator challenge 2	27
Calculator challenge 3	28
Making sequences and pattern spotting	28
Making triangle numbers	28
Card shuffle and logic	29
Half-time scores	29
Choose three numbers	29
The answer is 42	29

9 – Geometry unit

Name the triangles	30
Find all of the triangles on a 9-dot grid	31
Triangles and their areas	31
Triangles and their perimeters	31
Ordering perimeters as algebraic expressions	32
Find all of the quadrilaterals	32
Find all of the triangles on a 16 pin geoboard	32

Notes to accompany Geometry unit

Notes	33

1 – Addition and differencing

A Cuisenaire problem (addition)

Use all of these rods to make two equal lengths:

Look for more than one solution.

Making 10 (addition and partitioning)

Using three Cuisenaire rods we can make ten as follows:

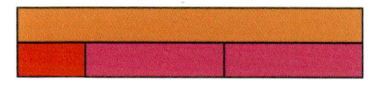

How many more ways are there of making ten from three rods?

For this puzzle these three arrangements are counted as the same.

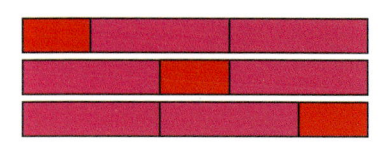

How many ways are there of making ten from four rods?

What about using five rods?

Coins (addition)

With just seven coins I can make every amount from 1p to 50p.

What are these coins? You can use more than one of each coin.

Show all your calculations.

If we allow eight coins, how far could you go?

Common triangle totals 1 (addition)

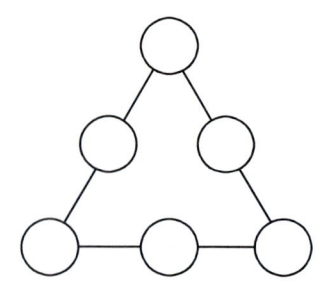

Arrange the numbers 1, 2, 3, 4, 5, 6 in the six circles so the sum of each line is 12.

What will be the common total and the arrangement if we use the numbers 4, 5, 6, 7, 8, 9?

What will be the common total and the arrangement if we use the numbers 5, 7, 9, 11, 13, 15?

Common triangle totals 2 (addition)

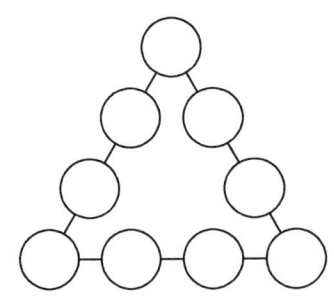

Place the numbers
1, 2, 3, 4, 5, 6, 7, 8, 9
in the circles so each side
of the triangle has a total of 17.

Dartboard totals

If all three darts hit the board, then
the smallest possible total will be 3
(i.e. 1+1+1)

The largest possible total will be 180
(i.e. treble 20 + treble 20 + treble 20)

What is the smallest total, after 3,
that cannot be made using three darts?

Domino challenge 1

A 3-3 set means the 10 dominoes formed when the highest number used is three. A 4-4 set has 15 dominoes and a 5-5 set has 21 dominoes.

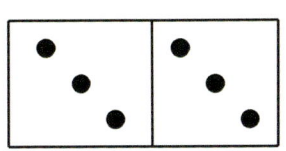

i) Using all the dominoes in a 3-3 set, partition them into five pairs so the total number of spots for each pair is the same.

ii) Using all the dominoes in a 3-3 set, try to make two groups of five dominoes so the total number of spots for each group is the same.

Domino challenge 2

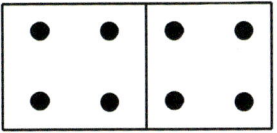

i) Using all the dominoes in a 4-4 set, partition them into three groups of five so the total number of spots for each set is the same.

ii) Partition a 4-4 set of dominoes into five groups of three, so the total number of spots in each group is the same.

iii) Group a 4-4 set of dominoes into a 5 by 3 array, so the rows of 5 dominoes each sum to the total for ii) AND the 3 columns of dominoes sum to the total in i).

Domino challenge 3

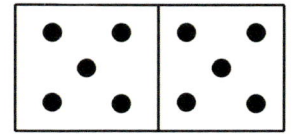

i) Partition a 5-5 set of dominoes into three equal groups so the total number of spots for each group is the same

ii) Partition a 5-5 set of dominoes into seven equal groups so the total number of spots for each group is the same.

Domino challenge 4

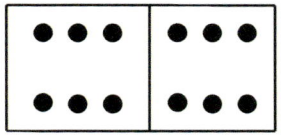

i) From a 6-6 set remove all the doubles and split it into seven equal groups so the total number of spots for each group is the same.

ii) From a 6-6 set remove all the doubles and split it into three equal groups so the total number of spots for each group is the same.

iii) Group a 6-6 set of dominoes, with the doubles removed, into a 7 by 3 array, so the rows of 7 dominoes each sum to the total in ii) AND the 3 columns of dominoes total to the total in i).

Dominoes and differencing 1

Choose whatever size of set you think will be appropriate for your pupils.

You might even use larger sets; a 7-7 set has 36 dominoes, an 8-8 set has 45 and a 9-9 set has 55 dominoes.

These games are to practise the idea of 'difference between' and pupils can work in groups of three.

The set of dominoes should be turned over, face down, and spread across a table.

Pupils take turns to:
- choose two dominoes
- find the total for each one
- find the difference between these two totals
- this value becomes their score for that 'go'
- the dominoes are not returned to the table

Players take turns and the 'winner' is the person with the greatest total of differences.

Clearly everyone will need to have the same number of turns so with some sets there will be some unused dominoes at the end of each game.

You could ask one member of the group to become the recorder of the scores for the other pair of players.

However each player should be encouraged to work out their scores, to be checked by the recorder.

Dominoes and differencing 2

The game could be made harder by interpreting the digits using place value.

For example if the two dominoes chosen are the [domino 1-3] and the [domino 2-1]

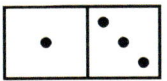

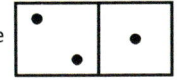

pupils have to turn these into two 2-digit numbers.

So as they appear above they would be worth 13 and 21 respectively, in which case the difference would be 8.

How would you arrange the dominoes in order to create the maximum difference?

Dominoes and differencing 3

This game involves multiplication and subtraction.

As before, pupils choose two of the face down dominoes and find the product of the numbers on each.
For example, for a 5-5 set, if the 5-3 and the 3-2 dominoes are chosen, the products are 15 and 6 so the resulting calculation will be 15 – 6 = 9. This game is also useful for practising multiplication by zero.

Maximum difference game

This is a game for 2 players.

Each player has two 3 by 1 grids.

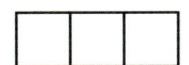

The digits from 0 to 9 are placed face down on the table and chosen at random and players have to decide where to place the numbers as each one appears.

Once a number has been chosen, it cannot be used again.

The idea is, that when six digits have been chosen placed in the grid, each player finds the (positive) difference.

The winner is the person with the largest difference.

Maximum product version

As before digits from 0 to 9 are chosen and players place each of five digits into each of the five spaces. The winner is the player who creates the largest product.

Pairing and squaring (Addition and recognising square numbers)

Arrange the numbers 3, 4, 5, 6, 10, 12, 13 and 15 so when adjacent numbers are added you always get a square total.

For example if I start with 13 I could place the 3 next to it.

This is because 13 + 3 = 16 and 16 is a square number (4 × 4)

I could also place the 12 next to the 13, because 13 + 12 = 25 and this is also a square number (5 × 5)

The challenge is to use all eight numbers.

Making amounts of money

Using 20p, 10p and 5p coins how many different ways are there to make 30p?

How many different ways are there to make 40p? 50p? 60p? ... £1?

Number grid problem (Addition and differencing)

Write the first twelve numbers 1, 2, 3, 4, 5, 6, 7, 8, 9, 10, 11, 12

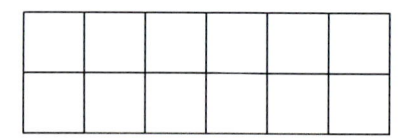

Place any six of these numbers in the top row of the grid in descending order, e.g.

10   7   6   4   2   1

Place the remaining six numbers in the 2nd row of the grid in ascending order, e.g.

10	7	6	4	2	1
3	5	8	9	11	12

Write the positive difference between each pair of numbers in the six columns, e.g.

10	7	6	4	2	1
3	5	8	9	11	12
7	2	2	5	9	11

Finally add together all the numbers in the 3rd row: 7 + 2 + 2 + 5 + 9 + 11 = ?

Explore what happens when you choose a different arrangement of the numbers. Remember the numbers in the top row are in descending order and those in the 2nd row are in ascending order.

Explore what happens if we started with the numbers 1,2,3,4,5,6,7,8,9,10.

2 – Number and Place Value

Number cards 1   (N&PV)

a) Use the following number cards to make five 2-digit numbers which are all even

| 0 | 1 | 2 | 3 | 4 | 5 | 6 | 7 | 8 | 9 |

b) It is also possible to make five 2-digit numbers which are all multiples of 9. What are they?

c) Now try to make another sequence of five 2-digit even numbers which ascend in equal size steps from the smallest to the largest.

Number cards 2   (N&PV)

Use the number cards 1, 2, 3 and 4 to make two 2-digit numbers then add them.

For example 31 + 24 = 55

How many different totals can you make?

What is the minimum?

What is the maximum?

Place your numbers in order from smallest to largest. What do you notice?

See what happens if you use 2, 3, 4 and 5… or 3, 4, 5 and 6… or

Reading numbers   (N&PV)

The number 12 345 in words is twelve thousand three hundred and forty five.

How do we write 654 321 in words?

What about 987 654 321?

Number of ones

Without looking at a 100 square, work out how many times the digit 1 appears.

What do all these ones total up to? (E.g. the one in 14 is worth 10)

Check your answers by looking at a 100 square.

Number cards 3 (N&PV)

Use these five number cards to make 2-digit numbers which are multiples of 3.

e.g. 30

| 0 | 1 | 2 | 3 | 4 |

How can you be sure you have found all possible solutions?

There are many more 3-digit number which are multiples of 3, (e.g. 312), see if you can find them all.

Number of millimetres (N&PV)

a) How many millimetres tall are you?

b) How many millimetres wide are you from finger tip to finger tip with your arms outstretched?

c) How many millimetres are there in 1 kilometre?

Strange but is it true? (N&PV)

Calculate the following:

a) 1 × 9 + 2 =

b) 12 × 9 + 3 =

c) 123 × 9 + 4 =

Predict what you think the next few answers will be?

Check to see if your predictions were correct.

Exponential growth (N&PV)

This is a problem to try out on someone at home!

Starting with 10p then doubling this to 20p on the next day and doubling this to 40p on the next day this means you will have 70p altogether after 3 days.

The sequence looks like this: 10p, 20p, 40p, ...

And the totals are: 10p, 30p, 70p, ...

If this doubling were to carry on for one week how much would you have by the end of the week?

How many days doubling would there need to be to go just beyond:

a) £100?

b) £1000?

c) £1M?

Working with decimals 1 (N & PV)

a) Write everything you understand about 0.1
b) Explain what you think the difference is between 0.1 and 0.10
c) Explain which is bigger, 0.31 or 0.4

Working with decimals 2 (N & PV)

Work with a partner of your choice.

Your challenge is to first discuss, then make a poster to describe everything you understand about the decimal point, what it is for and why it is an important part of learning mathematics.

Working with decimals 3 (N & PV)

Use the following number cards and the decimal point card to make all different possible numbers using all of these cards:

| 1 | 2 | 3 | . |

The only rule for this challenge is that the decimal point must be placed somewhere between two of the number cards.

For example you could make 21.3

| 2 | 1 | . | 3 |

Or you could make 2.31

| 2 | . | 3 | 1 |

a) How many different numbers can you make altogether?
b) Arrange your numbers in order from largest to smallest.
c) Find the difference between each pair of numbers when they are written in ascending order from smallest to largest.
d) What do all your differences total to?
e) Choose three of your own numbers and carry out parts a), b), c), d).
f) Write what you notice about the set of answers using 123 compared with the three numbers you chose.

3 – Mainly multiplication

A two dice problem

Throw two dice one after the other and record the number which appears.

In this example we have 46.

Your task is to identify which multiplication tables 46 is in and for each one you find to write a number sentence, e.g. 2 × 23 = 46.

Other than 23 × 2 = 46, are there any other multiplication number sentences for 46?

Listing factors

List all the numbers up to 100 which have exactly two factors.

List all the numbers up to 100 with an odd number of factors.

List the factors of numbers in the 'doubling from 1' sequence, i.e. 1, 2, 4, 8, 16, ... and explore how many factors there are.

What is the factor sum for each of the numbers in the 'doubling from 1' sequence?

Explore the factors of numbers in the 'tripling from 1' sequence.

Max Factor

List all the numbers us to 100 which have (say) more than six factors;

What number, up to 100, has the largest amount of factors.

Factor Chains

A factor chain is produced by adding together all the factors of a number, except for the number itself. For example, starting with 12, the sum of the factors except for 12 itself is {1 + 2 + 3 + 4 + 6}, i.e. 16.

Similarly, 16 generates a factor sum of 15 and the chain continues as follows:

$$12 \rightarrow 16 \rightarrow 15 \rightarrow 9 \rightarrow 4 \rightarrow 3 \rightarrow 1$$

The diagram below shows how some other numbers are connected together:

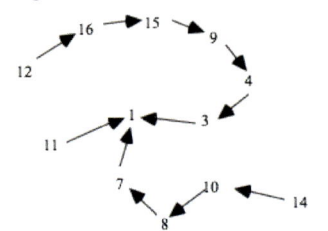

What number, less than 100, has the longest factor chain?

The highest LCM problem

This problem is about partitioning numbers into addition pairs, then working out the lowest common multiple for each pair, i.e.

Partitions of 10	LCM
9 and 1	9
8 and 2	8
7 and 3	21
6 and 4	12
5 and 5	5

When we partition 10 the highest LCM is 21.

The challenge is to explore the highest LCM when you partition other numbers.

Can you predict the highest LCM for any starting value?

Factors and consecutive sums

Explore connections between the factors of a number and what, and how many consecutive sums a number has.

For example, the factors of 15 are {1, 3, 5, 15}

There are three consecutive number sums for 15 and these are:

a) 7 + 8
b) 4 + 5 + 6
c) 1 + 2 + 3 + 4 + 5

Partitioning and multiplying

Find all of the ways of partitioning 17 into two numbers.

Take each pair of numbers and multiply them together.

For example if you choose 4 + 13 = 17 and calculate 4 × 13, the product is 52, because 4 × 13 = 52.

Which partition creates the largest product?

Suppose we partition 17 into three numbers.

What is the best partition to make the maximum product?

Multiplication facts

Write a list of the first ten multiples of 2.
Write a list of the first ten multiples of 3.
Write a list of the numbers which appear in **both** lists.

Find three numbers which are multiples of 4 **and** multiples of 3.
Find three numbers which are multiples of 5 **and** multiples of 3.
Find three numbers which are multiples of 7 **and** multiples of 3.
Find three numbers which are multiples of 6 **and** multiples of 4.
Find three numbers which are multiples of 6 **and** multiples of 9.
Find three numbers which are multiples of 4, multiples of 3 and multiples of 2.
Find three numbers which are multiples of 5, multiples of 3 and multiples of 2.

Multiplying consecutive numbers

The product of three consecutive numbers is 504.

What are the three numbers?

Make up some more calculations by multiplying three consecutive numbers together then give someone else your products for them to work out what your starting numbers were.

More multiplying consecutive numbers

Work out the answers to these four calculations:

$0 \times 1 =$
$1 \times 2 =$
$2 \times 3 =$
$3 \times 4 =$

Try to predict what the next four answers will be.
Check to see if you are correct.
Draw a graph of the first number in each multiplication as the x-coordinate and the product as the y-coordinate:
For example, (0, 0), (1, 2), (2, 6) etc.

Another multiplication marvel

Have a look at these calculations and check they are correct:

a) $5 \times 5 - 2 \times 2 = (5 + 2) \times (5 - 2)$
b) $3 \times 3 - 1 \times 1 = (3 + 1) \times (3 - 1)$
c) $7 \times 7 - 4 \times 4 = (7 + 4) \times (7 - 4)$
d) Make up some more of your own using the same structure.

Does it keep working? Try using some bigger numbers.

Largest product

Use the numbers 1, 2, 3, 4, 5 to make two numbers and multiply them together.

For example I could make

425 × 13 = 5525 ...

or I could make

4321 × 5 = 21605

Try to make two numbers with the largest possible product.

Which two numbers will make the smallest possible product?

Addition and multiplication

I have added together three numbers and my answer is 14.

When I multiply my three numbers together the product is 84.

What were my three numbers?

Make up some problem like this and display them on the wall.

Number of words in your current story book

Estimate how many words there are from the beginning to the end of your current story book.

You are not intended to count every word!

However, you must show what you have done to make your estimate.

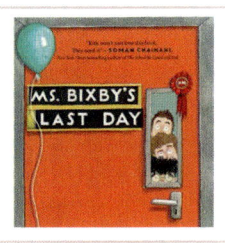

Birth Date Values

A birth date value is made by finding the product of the day in the month and the number of the month in a year. So if a birth date is 5th June, the calculation is 5 × 6 and the BDV is 30.

Who else in a class has the same BDV but not the same birth date? As it happens 30 is a BDV rich number because the following birth dates will be equal to 30: 30th January, 15th February and several more. Clearly not all BDVs are unique.

If we know a person's BDV can we calculate their possible birth date?

Some further questions might be:
- Which BDVs are unique
- What are the minimum and the maximum BDVs in a class?
- Which BDVs have the most birth dates?
- What values between minimum and maximum BDVs cannot be made?
- What is the largest prime BDV?
- Which dates give BDVs which are square numbers
- Which dates are triangular BDVs?
- In a group of people who has the average BDV?

What other problems can you devise based upon BDVs?

4 – Number chains

Number chain 1

Here is a number chain:

$$39 \rightarrow 27 \rightarrow 14 \rightarrow 4$$

Try to work out how the chain has been formed.

Once you know the 'rule', choose a different starting number to make a longer number chain.

Number chain 2   Happy Numbers

A happy number works like this.

Start with a number, say 28.

Now calculate $2^2 + 8^2 = 4 + 64$.

And $4 + 64 = 68$.

Now repeat with 68, $6^2 + 8^2 = 100$.

Now repeat with 100, $1^2 + 0^2 + 0^2 = 1$.

We now have the following number chain.

Number chains that end in 1 are said to be happy numbers:

$$28 \rightarrow 68 \rightarrow 100 \rightarrow 1$$

See how many more happy numbers you can find up to 100.

Number chain 3

You will need a copy of a 100 grid so you can colour in the numbers which appear in a chain to keep a record of those you have used.

For this chain choose a 2-digit number, multiply the unit digit by 4 and add on the tens digit.

Starting with 28 the next number is $8 \times 4 + 2 = 34$

Here is a chain starting at 28:

$$28 \rightarrow 34 \rightarrow 19 \rightarrow 37 \rightarrow \dots$$

Continue this chain and see what happens.

Use your 100 grid and keep track of the numbers in your chains.

Number chain 4

Choose a number.

If your number is even then halve it.

If you number is odd then subtract 1.

Continue in this way until you reach the number 1.

So, starting with 11 the chain would look like this:

$$11 \rightarrow 10 \rightarrow 5 \rightarrow 4 \rightarrow 2 \rightarrow 1$$

Make some of your own chains by choosing different starting numbers.

What is the longest chain you can have with a starting number up to 50?

What is the longest chain you can find up to 100?

5 – Calculations using +, –, ×, ÷ and brackets

Making up calculations 1 [+, –, ×, ÷ and brackets]

Starting with the number 4 make up a calculation using only the number 4 together with +, –, × and ÷ and brackets to gain the answer of 9.

Here is one way of doing it:

$$4 \times 4 - 4 - 4 + 4 \div 4 = 9$$

Can you find a shorter way?

Suppose we could only use the number 3 together with +, –, × and ÷ and brackets, how could you make 11?

Make up some more of your own challenges, e.g. only using 5 and ending up with 3.

Making up calculations 2 [+, –, ×, ÷ and brackets]

This problem is about using five 5s to make all possible answers from 1 upwards.

I have allowed the use of 55 and 5! which is a shorthand for $5 \times 4 \times 3 \times 2 \times 1$ and is equal to 120.

So far I have worked out solutions for all the counting numbers up to 22; each time using five 5s for each value.

There may be more than one way of reaching the same number, for example, below are two ways of gaining the answer of 10:

  i) $5 \times 5 - 5 - 5 - 5 = 10$
  ii) $55 \div 5 - 5 \div 5 = 10$

Making up calculations 3   [+, −, ×, ÷ and brackets]

Calculate:

a) 2 + 4 × 5 + 3

b) (2 + 4) × 5 + 3

c) 2 + 4 × (5 + 3)

d) (2 + 4) × (5 + 3)

What answers do you get if the + 3 is changed to − 3?

Make up some of calculations yourself using four different numbers.

Calculate your answers then ask someone else to work them out and see if they get the same answers.

Making up calculations 4   [+, −, ×, ÷ and brackets]

Make up some of calculations yourself using five different numbers.

Work out your answers then ask someone else to work them out and see if they get the same answers, e.g. 6 + 4 ÷ 2 + 3 × 5 (My, correct answer is 23).

Six 6s   [+, −, ×, ÷ and brackets]

Using six 6s make all the counting numbers as far as you can go from 1 upwards.

For example (66 − 6 × 6) ÷ 6 + 6 = 11

Seven 7s   [+, −, × and ÷, brackets]

Using seven 7s make all the counting numbers as far as you can go from 1 upwards.

For example [(7 × 7 + 7 × 7) + 7] ÷ 7 + 7 = 22

The four dice challenge [+, −, × and ÷, brackets]

Throw four dice and use the uppermost values as single digit numbers. The idea is to use all four numbers, in any order, and once each together with any of the four operations. These can be used more than once, as well as brackets.

The task is to see how far you can go without missing out any values from zero upwards. The example below is based upon throwing: 1, 3, 5 and 3.

Calculation	Target	Calculation	Target
	= 0		= 15
	= 1		= 16
	= 2	3 + 5 × 3 − 1*	= 17
	= 3		= 18
	= 4		= 19
	= 5		= 20
	= 6		= 21
	= 7		= 22
	= 8		= 23
	= 9	(5 + 3) × (1 + 3)	= 24
	= 10		= 25
	= 11		= 26
5 + 3 + 3 + 1 (Easy-peasy)	= 12		= 27
	= 13		= 28
	= 14		= 29

* Note this calculation makes 17 and not 23.

For it to make 23 we would need to use brackets and write the calculation as: (3 + 5) × 3 − 1

Can all the values up to 29 be found?

Can you go beyond 29?

6 – Measures

Digital clocks

On a digital clock there are some times which have a special property.
This is when the minutes digits add up to the hours digits.
For example 7:25 (so 2+5 = 7) and 13:49 (so 4+9 = 13)
Which hour has the most of these times?

One-handed clocks   (Measures)

Here are some clocks which only have the hour hand on each face.
What are the approximate times on the following page?
Having estimated these times draw in the minute hand.

20

Times before noon

How many times are there between 00:00 and 12:00 when the sum of the digits is 15.
For example 02:58 (So 0+2+5+8 = 15)

Distance around your head

Measure the distance around your head.
Multiply this distance by 3
How close is this to your height?

Height and arm span

What is the difference, in centimetres, between your height and your arm span?

Middle of a year

What date is exactly in the middle of a year containing 365 days?

I have a good friend who lives in Falmouth

Where is Falmouth?
How far is it from Grayrigg to Falmouth?
How long do you think it would take to drive to Falmouth from Grayrigg?
How long would it take to get to Falmouth on a train from Oxenholme Station?

Scale drawing

Make a scale drawing of your classroom which is ten times smaller than the actual room.

Time

Work out how many minutes there are in one year.

How many minutes old will you be by the time you have finished this calculation?

Date and time

Write down today's date and the time it is now, to the nearest minute.

What will be the day, the date and the time in exactly 100 hours?

What will the answer be in 1000 hours?

Weighing things up

Which is worth most, one kilogram of 1p coins.
or half a kilogram of 2p coins?

How much is your name worth?

Emma's name is worth 32p.

Samara's name is worth 52p.

Lizzie's name worth 87p and Henry's name is worth 70p.

How much is your name worth?

What is the total value of the first names of the children in your class?

What is the average value of the first names of all the children in your class?

Weight of water

One cubic metre of water weighs 1 tonne.

Estimate the weight of water in a swimming pool.

One million minutes

How old, to the nearest week, is someone who has lived one million minutes?

How many minutes old will you be on your next birthday?

A hearty question

The average heart pumps 4 litres of blood per minute.

How many litres is this each day?

How many gallons is this each day?

Hour and minute hands

What times are the hour hand and the minute hand at an angle of 180° to each other?

Try to write your answers to the nearest minute.

By the way, quarter past nine is not a correct answer!

7 – Algebra

Think of a number

I have thought of a number.
I have multiplied it by 2.
I have added 3 to the total.
My answer is 17.
What number did I start with?

Make up some of your own puzzles like this, involving:
Multiplying and adding, **for others to solve**
Multiplying and subtracting
Adding and multiplying
Subtracting and multiplying

Make up some of your own puzzles like this involving adding and multiplying then subtracting.

For example:
I have thought of a number
I have added 5
I have multiplied the total by 3
I have subtracted 7
The answer is 26
What number did I start with?

Algebra and addition 1

I have thought of three different numbers a, b and c which are all less than ten.

When I work out $a + b$ the answer is 8.

When I work out $b + c$ the answer is 13.

When I work out $a + c$ the answer is 11.

What were my three numbers?

Make up a problem like this for a partner to solve.
You might agree to have bigger numbers, for instance where all three numbers are <20 or are all <50.

Algebra and addition 2

I have thought of three consecutive numbers p, q and r all less than ten.

When I add $p + q + q + r + p + r$ the answer is 42.

What were my numbers?

Make up a problem like this for a partner to solve.
You might agree to have bigger numbers, for instance where all three numbers are <20 or are <50.

Algebra and fractions

The area of the whole square is 1.

What are the areas of each of the pieces A, B, C ..., F?

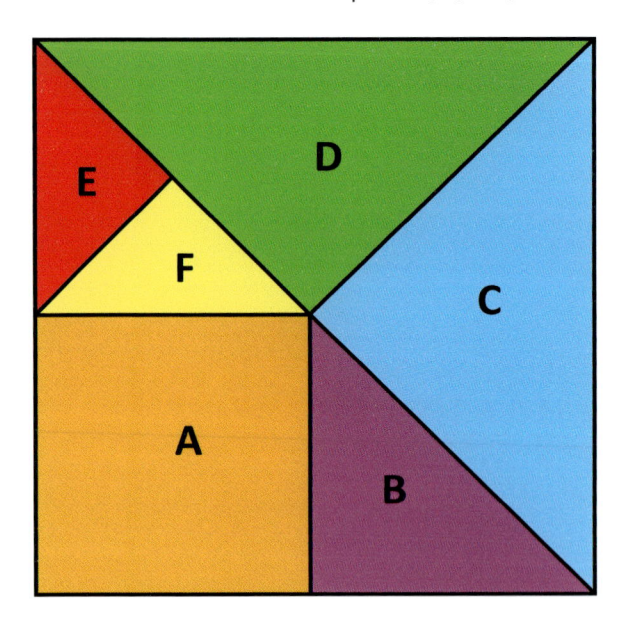

Make up some area equations such as A + B + C = ...

Or some missing letter equations such as C + B + ... = ...

8 – Miscellany

Making 5 (Sequencing and being systematic)

Using white and/or red rods only here are some ways of making the same length as yellow:

How many more ways can you find?

My list of arrangements is not very mathematical because I have not used a systematic method.

Try to arrange all your results in a more systematic way and a much better one than mine!

Explore how many ways there are of making other colours by only using white and/or red rods.

Making 15

Using three different numbers and addition only, how many ways can you make 15?

For example:

1 + 5 + 9 = 15

See if you can make a systematic list so you can show you have found all possible solutions.

If we turn each set of three numbers into the dimensions of a cuboid:
- Which three numbers make a cuboid with the largest volume?
- Calculate the surface areas of each of the cuboids you have made.
- Which dimensions make the smallest and largest surface areas?

Cuisenaire and area

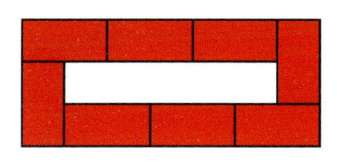

a) Here is a rectangle made from 8 red rods.
   It has an outside area of 16 and inside area of 5.
   How many more different rectangles can you make from eight red rods?
   What do you notice about the outside and the inside areas of your rectangles?

b) How many different rectangles can be made from 10 red rods?
   What about 12 red rods?
   What about 14 red rods … ?

c) What about six green rods?
   What about 8 green rods … ?

Dominoes and the game of 3s and 2s

This is a simpler version of the game of 5s and 3s described below and could be played with a 4-4 set of dominoes.

In this variation points are scored when the 'end values' total to a multiple of either 2 or 3.

Thus if the end values total to 12, this would score six (for the 2s) and four (for the 3s) making a total of ten points.

Similarly if the end values total to 6, this would score three (2s) and two (3s) making a total of 5.

Dominoes and the game of 5s and 3s

The basic idea is to play dominoes by matching pairs of the same numbers and adding together the values appearing at either **end**. Players score points according to whether the 'end' total is divisible by either 5 and/or 3.

'Doubles' are placed 'vertically' rather than horizontally.

Below is the beginning of a game between two players A and B:

If **player A** plays [5-4 domino] this scores 3 points because $(5 + 4) \div 3 = 3$

If **player B** adds the 6-5 domino to form the following arrangement:

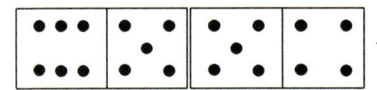

[6-5, 5-4 dominoes] this gives a score of 2 because $(6 + 4) \div 5 = 2$ (points)

If **player A** now plays the 4-3 this will give a score of 3:

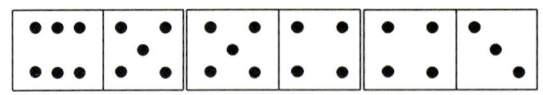

[6-5, 5-4, 4-3 dominoes] This is because $(6 + 3) \div 3 = 3$ (points)

Scores are accumulated so **player A** at this point of the game has scored a total of 6 points.

If **player B** now plays the double 6 this is placed 'vertically', as shown below and the two ends now total to 15 (i.e. 6 + 6 + 3).

In fact all doubles are placed vertically.

In this situation **Player B** scores 8 points for making a total of 15 because 15 divides by both 5 and 3, so $15 \div 5 = 3$ (points) and $15 \div 3 = 5$ (points), e.g.:

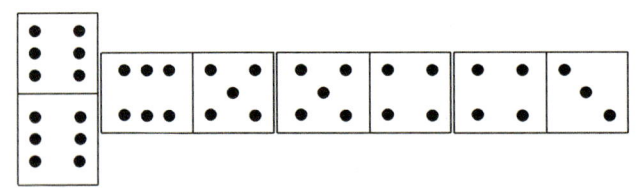

[double-6, 6-5, 5-4, 4-3 dominoes]

The game continues and the winner is the person to score 121 points (or twice around a *cribbage* board).

Guzintas (What goes into...)

What are the factors of 10? How many factors does 10 have?
What are the factors of 100? How many factors does 100 have?
What are the factors of 1000? How many factors does 1000 have?
What are the factors of 10000? How many factors does 10000 have?

Summing consecutive numbers

6, 7 and 8 are three consecutive numbers.
Their sum is 6 + 7 + 8 = 21.
Can you find three consecutive numbers whose sum is:
 a) 12?
 b) 27?
 c) 39?
Try to find a quick way of working out the sum of ANY three consecutive numbers.
Explain why 50 cannot be the sum of three consecutive numbers.

Calculator challenge 1

When I divide the number 1234 by 11, I do not get a whole number answer.
However if I rearrange the number 1234 to 2431, do I get a whole number when I divide this new number by 11. (i.e. 2431 ÷ 11 = 221).
Find many different ways can rearrange the digits 1234 so when you divide your new number by 11 you get a whole number answer.

Calculator challenge 2

Use a calculator to find the missing numbers in this calculation:

Try to find more pairs of missing numbers to get the same answer of 0.4.
Find some pairs of numbers so the answer is 2.5.

$$\square \div \bigcirc = 2.5$$

Find some pairs of numbers so the answer is 0.8.
Find some pairs of numbers so the answer is 1.25.

Calculator challenge 3

Choose a 1-digit number, divide it by 11 and write down the answer.

Explore what answers you gain by dividing other 1-digit numbers by 11.

What happens when you divide 2-digit numbers by 11?

Making sequences and pattern spotting

Starting with any two numbers develop a sequence that is made by doubling the first number and adding the next.

So starting with 2 and 3 the next number is 7 because $2 \times 2 + 3 = 7$.

We know have three numbers in the sequence: 2, 3, 7

To find the next number I double the 3 then add 7, so the next number will be $3 \times 2 + 7 = 13$.

The sequence now looks like this 2, 3, 7, 13.

   a) Find the next four numbers in the sequence.

   b) What patterns do you notice?

   c) This is a really hard question.
      What are the three numbers before the 2 when the sequence is reversed, i.e. 13, 7, 3, 2, ?, ?, ?,

Make up your own sequences by choosing the first two numbers.

You might for example start with 3, 2, ...

Making triangle numbers (Sequences & pattern spotting)

A triangle number is made using patterns of counters which fit inside a triangle.

Here are the first three triangle numbers: 1, 3 and 6.

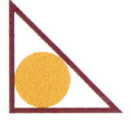

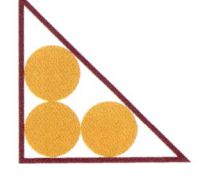

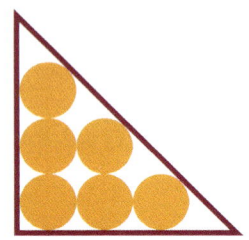

   a) Make the next seven triangle numbers.

   b) Explore what happens when you add any adjacent pair of triangle numbers together.

   c) Explore what happens when you multiply each triangle number by 8 and add 1.

Card Shuffle and logic

This challenge is based upon the following 'shuffle':

- Place the first card face down on the table
- Put the second card on the bottom of the pack
- Place the third card on top of the first card
- Put the fourth card on the bottom of the pack
- Place the fifth card on top of the third card
- Continue until all 8 cards are face down on top of each other on the table.

The challenge is to decide how to arrange the cards before you do the shuffle, so when you turn them over you see this arrangement.

Half-time scores (Logic)

The final score for a game was 2-1.

What different scores could there have been at half-time?

Explore different possible half-time scores for different full-time scores.

Choose three numbers   (Coordinates and area)

Choose three numbers e, f and g in ascending order and all less than ten.

Pair them together to form three coordinate pairs: (e, f), (f, g) and (e, g).

Plot your points on 1cm squared paper.

What type of shape is formed?

What is the area of your shape?

What happens if I plot the coordinates the other way round (f, e), (g, f) and (g, e)?

The answer is 42

Make up some questions so the answer is 42.

9 – Geometry unit *See notes to accompany this unit on pages 33 to 35*

Name the triangles

You may wish to cut out these triangles:

Your challenge is to name the triangles using these five names:

  a) Scalene

  b) Scalene & right-angled

  c) Isosceles

  d) Isosceles & right-angled

  e) Equilateral

Find all of the triangles on a 9-dot grid

How many times can each of the eight triangles be made in different places on the geoboard? For example the scalene triangle below can be made eight times as follows:

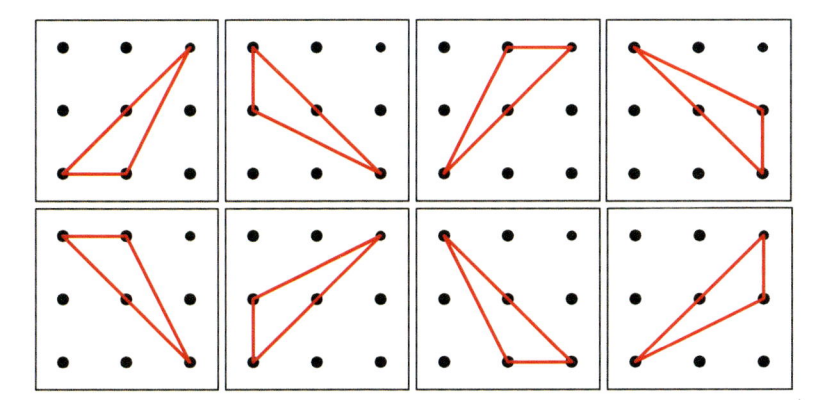

Altogether there are a total of 76 congruences of the 8 possible triangles.

Triangles and their areas

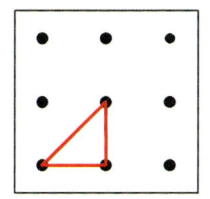

The area of this triangle is half of a square unit

Try to calculate the areas of your other triangles.

Triangles and their perimeters

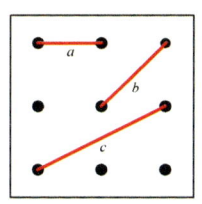

This challenge is to work out the perimeters of your triangles in an algebraic way.

You are given the following information about three of the different lengths, a, b and c that can be made on a 9-pin geoboard.

As an example, the triangle below is made from two 'a' lengths and one 'b' length so its perimeter, written algebraically, is $P = a + a + b$. This can be shortened to $P = 2a + b$.

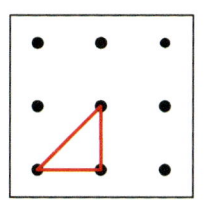

Ordering perimeters as algebraic expressions

Use the following statement: $a < b < c$ about the different lengths a, b and c from 'Triangles and their perimeters'.

Your challenge is to put your eight perimeters in order of length from the shortest to the longest.

Find all of the quadrilaterals

How many different quadrilaterals can you find on a 9-pin geoboard?

When you think you have found them all, calculate their areas and perimeters.

Find all of the triangles on a 16 pin geoboard

How many **new**, non-congruent triangles can you make on a 16-pin geoboard?

This is quite a difficult challenge as there are more than twenty such triangles.

Work out the areas of your triangles.

To work out the perimeters of these triangles you will need to use two new, different lengths.

These are labelled d and e as in the diagram below:

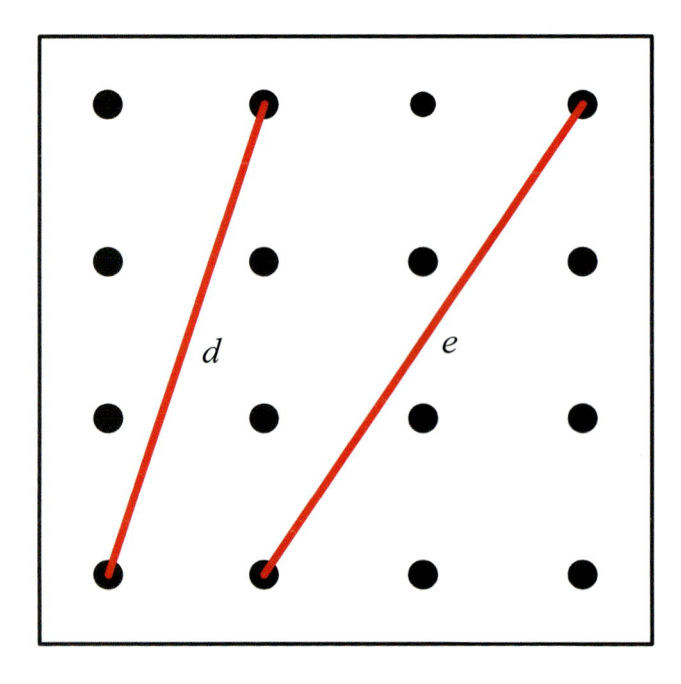

Notes to accompany Geometry unit

This unit begins with everyone exploring how many different triangles can be made on a square 9-pin geoboard. Following this exploration there are two whole class tasks about finding them all and discussing their properties and names as follows:

Problems based upon a 9-pin geoboard

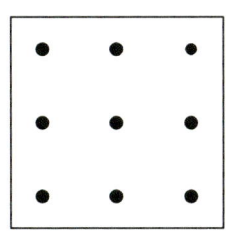

a) Finding all the possible different (non-congruent) triangles.

b) Discussing and describing their properties in terms of equal lengths of sides, right-angles, line symmetry and aligning these properties to their names.

Note that on any square dot grid, it is not possible to make an equilateral triangle; the proof of this would require 'GCSE level' reasoning.

Name the triangles

This is effectively a worksheet, which needs a pair of scissors taking to it! It may be omitted by some children. When I used it, I said it was an optional task for those children who were not sure about the names of different types of triangles.

Find all of the triangles

This is about looking for, and describing, the transformations of each of the eight different triangles to make all the other triangles that are congruent to it. I suggest all children attempt this challenge. Once everyone has attempted it you may wish to discuss it with the class as a whole, introducing the language of reflection, translation and rotation. The example shown in 'Find all of the triangles' does not have any translations, however the following example shows one that does:

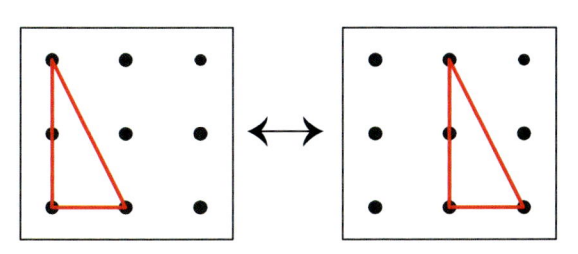

'Congruence' is an important idea in geometry and so it is important to model using the word and encourage children to use it when describing shapes.

Triangles and their areas

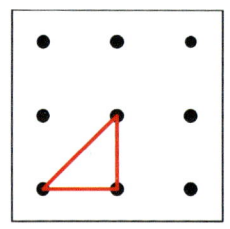

Ask learners to calculate the areas of the eight triangles, given that the area of the one shown on the left is half a unit square.

A useful discussion to have with those children who are 'ready' to engage with a slightly more complex idea is that of working out the area of a shape by drawing a rectangle around it. Then discuss and calculate the 'outside' areas and subtract this from the area of the whole rectangle.

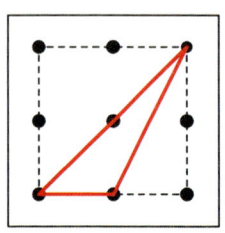

Note the 'rectangle' referred to, previously, is, in this instance, a square.

Triangles and their perimeters

This is looking at the perimeters, algebraically, using the following coding for three different lengths:

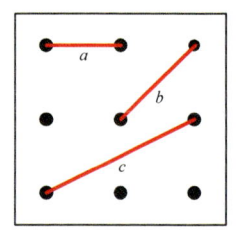

Ordering perimeters as algebraic expressions

This is about algebraically arranging the perimeters of the eight triangles in order of length from shortest to longest given the statement $a<b<c$.

Find all of the quadrilaterals

This is about finding all possible quadrilaterals on a 9-pin geoboard, naming them, calculating their areas and their perimeters using the same coding system as for *'Triangles and their perimeters'*.

The complete set of quadrilaterals is shown below:

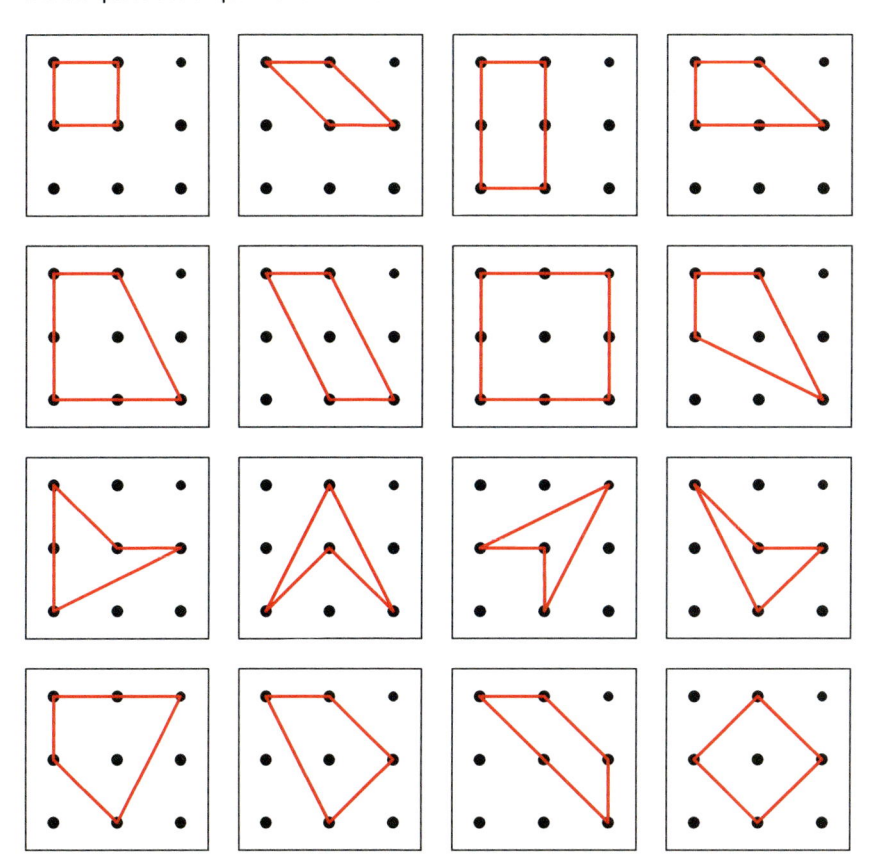

Find all the triangles on a 16-pin geoboard

This is to explore new triangles on a 16-pin grid and then to apply the same knowledge about names, properties, areas and perimeters of these triangles.

Mike's 100 square grid (available as download and included with PDF)

91	92	93	94	95	96	97	98	99	100
81	82	83	84	85	86	87	88	89	90
71	72	73	74	75	76	77	78	79	80
61	62	63	64	65	66	67	68	69	70
51	52	53	54	55	56	57	58	59	60
41	42	43	44	45	46	47	48	49	50
31	32	33	34	35	36	37	38	39	40
21	22	23	24	25	26	27	28	29	30
11	12	13	14	15	16	17	18	19	20
1	2	3	4	5	6	7	8	9	10

Mike's 9 dot x 12 grid (available as download and included with PDF)

About this Book

Pick and Mix
Mathematical Challenges for a KS2 classroom

ISBN 978 1 898611 99 8

Association of Teachers of Mathematics

Vernon House
2A Vernon Street
Derby DE1 1FR

Acknowledgement

Thank you to the pupils and staff at Grayrigg C of E Primary School, Cumbria, with whom the activities, challenges and methodology used in this book have been piloted.

This book is accompanied by a PDF document for use in the classroom.

Published April 2017

Printed in England

Copyright

©2017 Association of Teachers of Mathematics

All rights reserved

The whole of the book and PDF is subject to copyright and permission is granted for the pages to be reproduced for use in the purchasing institution or by the purchasing individual only.

Further copies of this book may be purchased from the previous address